GOSPEL X
- Multiplying the message

Imprint

CONTRIBUTING AUTHORS:
Stephan Pues
Tim Coomar
Neil Powell
Alexander Deuscher
Maria Boschker

EDITORS:
Andreas West
Maria Boschker

© 2024 Exponential Europe e.V.
Grüne Trift 28a, 12557 Berlin
exponential.eu
mail@exponential.eu

All rights reserved. Reproduction of this book or parts thereof is not permissible under current German copyright law, unless expressly given by the author(s).

DESIGN AND LAYOUT:
Pierre Dinger
Andreas West

This book uses the New International Version - UK as the common Bible translation unless referenced otherwise.

Introduction	*4*
The Setup of the Workbook	*12*
Session 1: The Value of the Gospel	*14*
Session 2: The Value of Multiplication of the Gospel	*18*
Session 3: The Language of the Gospel	*22*
Session 4: The Behaviour of the Gospel	*26*
Session 5: Commitment to Multiplying the Gospel	*30*
Next Steps	*34*
Going Deeper	*38*
Partners	*76*

Introduction

Exponential Europe's vision is to see reproduction and multiplication being the norm in the language and behaviour of the church in Europe. We want to see reproduction and multiplication of the gospel, disciples, leaders, communities, churches and networks. Many churches in Europe are declining, some plateauing and some are growing. What would it look like if 10% of all the churches in your city, your denomination or organisation started to plant new churches, or reproduce the gospel, disciples, and leaders on all levels? We want to see churches come to a place of reproduction and multiplication. We want to see Multipliers who are healthy disciple-making leaders, who champion reproduction. Exponential is a community with a cause with leaders from all of Europe with a dream to see reproduction and multiplication being the norm in the language and behaviour of the church in Europe.

Our 2024 topic is Gospel X - multiplying the message. Jesus left the church the vision of a movement when he challenged us to reproduce from our own Jerusalem into *'all Judea and Samaria, and to the ends of the earth'* (Acts 1:8). For us to see a movement, we need every Christ follower to adopt Jesus' personal mission to *'seek and to save the lost'* (Luke 19:10). Evangelism is core to the mission of Jesus and essential to accomplishing his vision.

Culture of Evangelism

The State of Evangelism in Europe

For a better understanding about the state of Evangelism in Europe, we recommend reading the report: **Europe 2021 - A Missiological Report** by Jim Memory. Europe is very diverse in culture and language. We have the Catholic south, the protestant north, the Orthodox East, and the mixed Balkan. The strength in the gospel presence is also very different from nation to nation and region to region in the European context.

The biggest difference is probably the predominantly Catholic and Orthodox countries of Eastern and Southern Europe compared to the Protestant North. As Protestantism did not take root to the same extent in the Southern and Eastern regions, the Church there kept its status quo for a longer time. Once people started to leave the churches, the reaction of the Church in the South and East was to focus on being missional again. The churches of the Protestant North however welcomed the Church Growth Theology in the 1970s. Churches started to do church in such a way to keep people in the church. As a result, the 'form' was overemphasised compared to the 'content'. What we need now goes deeper than Church Growth philosophy of strategy and leadership. We need a fresh understanding of the power of the gospel and how it can be spread and renewed in a European context.

Talking about Evangelism in one way for the whole of Europe is therefore a tremendous task and we believe it will be important for each nation and region to gain a deeper understanding of their context and communicate this in an Exponential Regional or Exponential Roundtable.

What we have in common is that we all need to work with the question: How can we see both the message and the messenger being multiplied across the European context? Most of our nations are in an increasing secularisation, and we need to take a deeper look at the gospel.

In Europe, we have seen local churches and ministries bring the gospel out to new people in various ways. We see evangelism-oriented churches growing that focus on the people outside the church. A variety of student ministries have been used with great success. Alpha Course is one of the most used tools for evangelism in the church of Europe and with all the immigrants coming into Europe, we see a new seal of evangelistic passion. They are among the most growing churches in Europe. Some churches emphasise strong social involvement as a means to reach new people.

In order to see multiplication of the gospel, people need to be inspired by the

local stories and develop a language and understanding of the gospel that goes deeper than methods and strategies. We need a fresh understanding of the power of the gospel and how it can be spread and renewed in a European context.

This is the main focus of *Gospel X*. Below you can read more about the five sessions that will take place in all Exponential Regionals and Roundtables. The two first sessions emphasise *the values*: **The Gospel** and **The Multiplication of the Gospel**. The goal is to give a fresh biblical understanding. The third session emphasises *the narrative*: **Where and what are the stories in the different contexts that embodies what we want to see?** The fourth session is all about *behaviour*: **What change in our behaviour is needed to see a new gospel movement in Europe?** The final session is *commission*: **Sending people out to do it**.

NOTES

Session #1: The Gospel

There is a need for a fresh understanding of the power of the gospel and how it can be spread and renewed in a European context. As we have mentioned there are differences in Europe, but today the gospel seems not clear for many.

Romans 5:8 tells us that *'God demonstrates his own love for us in this, while we were still sinners, Christ died for us'*. While we were still in the process of rejecting him, God was persistently pursuing us in the person of Jesus. He was on mission to restore a broken relationship with each of us. Lost people matter to God and he desires that all of us come to know him (God is patient…*'not wanting anyone to perish, but for everyone to come to repentance'* (2 Peter 3:9)). We are all prodigals. God wants us to find our way back to him and our eternal home. Our commitment to the gospel begins when we make it personal. We are all lost people! When we let that truth motivate us, we can't help but be passionate about reaching people far from God. In his book, Movements, Steve Addison reminds us that the movements that change the world are missionary movements of Christ followers with a white-hot faith. The same love that stirred God to sacrifice his son for us should stir inside each of us for a lost world. We should each adopt Jesus' mission as our own personal mission: *'to seek and to save the lost'* (Luke 19:10). It was because of that mission Jesus went out of his way to get to know Zacchaeus and ultimately brought salvation to his house. And here is what happens when we have that kind of passion for the gospel: *'And each day the Lord added to their fellowship those who were being saved'* (Acts 2:47 NLT). As leaders who are passionate about the gospel the only thing that will matter is making sure that the lost are found. As a result of that passion, we will commit to starting new churches with evangelistic cultures, knowing this is the best way to reach a lost world. A church with a culture of evangelism will hold the Biblical values of evangelism, share the compelling narratives of evangelism, and live out the white-hot faith behaviours of an evangelistic church.

Session #2: Multiplying the Gospel

The soil of Europe is different from nation to nation. In the last years, we have seen revival among the Gypsy in Europe, the gospel has impacted the poor and the marginalised and we have seen a revival among the alcoholic and drug addicts in the Pentecostal movement in Europe, especially in Ukraine. There is a strong immigrant influence in Europe.

Mark 4 tells us the parable of the seed. The seed falls on four different grounds; the way, the rocks, the thorns, and the soil. Depending on where the seed falls, the seed will generate a big harvest or little or no harvest. This parable teaches us that not all the seeds sown will produce fruit. Only some of the seeds we sow will also result in the gospel taking root in a person's life. Statistically speaking, only a fourth of our sowing will result in a harvest. Practically, missiologist Frog Owing once stated, we need to share the gospel with 50 000 people to harvest 500 people. How can we be confident in sharing the message of Christ with more people? If we need to increase the gospel exposure, we want to see a harvest of people coming to faith. How can we do this? What is needed to reach many more people with the gospel? What are our practices today and what needs to be changed?

Furthermore, we need to ask ourselves:

» *What are the barriers to the multiplication of the gospel?*

» *What are the ways, the rocks, and the thorns in our countries?*

» *What are the concerns, the troubles of today that hinder people from receiving the gospel?*

Session #3:
Everyone shares everywhere

Imagine if everyone shared the gospel everywhere. Words matter. Whoever owns the language will ultimately create the culture. If we are to create a culture of evangelism then we must be intentional about creating and consistently using language that will mobilise Christians to reach lost people. The language around evangelism is hospitality, disciple-making, friendship, influence, and invitation. It is about companionship, challenge, opportunity, conversation, and something you get-to-do. The writer of Hebrews challenges us, *'Do not forget to show hospitality to strangers…'* (Hebrews 13:2). When Paul explains to believers how to put love into action he says, *'Share with the Lord's people who are in need. Practice hospitality'* (Romans 12:13). Peter also chimes in, *'Offer hospitality to one another without grumbling'* (1 Peter 4:9). Once we have invited people into our homes, we can ask for their stories, listen to them and then also tell our stories.

Storytelling is a powerful way to encapsulate values and reinforce the desired behaviours in culture creation. In creating a culture of evangelism, we need to share accounts of people who love and lead others to follow Jesus, that show us how it can be done and make us believe we can do it. In Luke 15 Jesus tells three of the best short stories ever told; the story of the lost sheep, the lost coin, and the lost son. In each of the stories Jesus reinforces the value of what is lost over what is found, the priority of searching, and the celebration of when the lost is found. If we are to lead in creating a culture of evangelism we must tell our own stories, tell the stories of our community, share stories of others to inspire us to live out Jesus' mission to 'seek and save the lost,' and expose our listeners to the beauty of the Biblical text (seeker Bible studies).

Session #4: Multiplying the message

We started by saying that Europe is very diverse in culture and language. We believe that each region and nations need to adapt and give answers to the question how the gospel can be multiplied in their context. Each region needs to come up with their stories. In general, we believe a culture of generosity and hospitality will be key for reaching people with the gospel. The B.L.E.S.S. practice is a good way of exploring hospitality. The Jesus Creed can be summarised as *'Love God and love your neighbour'* (Matthew 22:37-38). Jesus earned the nickname *'friend of sinners'* (Luke 7:34), because he loved his neighbours the way they wanted to be loved. For us to create a culture of evangelism we too will risk being called friends of sinners and become people who love our neighbours.

Contextualisation of this is different in the many cultures in Europe. When we come to the workshop we tailor the workshop to the different focus on Evangelism with the integration of different hospitality practices.

At the same time, in Europe more methods and ministries seek to reach the lost in their way. We have media evangelism, street evangelism, and more diaconal evangelism. Alpha Course is one of the most impacting tools for evangelism in Europe for the last 30 years. The question we want to answer is: What is the best praxis of gospel multiplication in your context? What are the stories and how did it happen?

Session #5: Think Big!

Jesus left the church his vision of a movement when he challenged us to reproduce from our own Jerusalem into *'all Judea and Samaria, and the ends of the earth'* (Acts 1:8). For us to see a movement we need every Christ follower to adopt Jesus' personal mission to *'seek and to save the lost'* (Luke 19:10). This will be accomplished by communities of believers with white-hot evangelistic cultures that are known for loving and blessing their neighbours.

Some of Jesus' last instructions to his followers were to *'go and make disciples of all nations, baptising them in the name of the Father and of the Son and of the Holy Spirit, and teaching them to obey everything I have commanded you. And surely I am with you always, to the very end of the age'* (Matthew 28:19-20).

Throughout the centuries, there have been revivals and movements in Europe. Can this happen again? What is the first step we have to take for this to become reality? What hinders us from taking the next step? What do we need to do to overcome this hindrance?

There is a connection between sowing the gospel, welcoming new converts, and planting new churches. How can we utilise the parable of the seed from Mark 4 to create an overflow of evangelism?

About
The Setup of the Workbook

1. An introduction to Exponential Europe and the theme of Gospel X.

2. Five sessions with the same structure – two action items for each individual session:
   - Watch the input video.
   - Discuss the questions around tables.
   - Use the Notes section for reflections, questions and ideas.

3. An overview of, as well as opportunities for your *Next Steps* in the Exponential journey.

4. *Going Deeper*: A deeper dive into this year's theme, written by different authors, created to help you in your onward journey after Roundtables.

> **This workbook is divided into 5 sessions:**
>
> SESSION 1 IS ABOUT
> THE **VALUE** OF THE GOSPEL.
>
> SESSION 2 IS ABOUT
> THE **VALUE OF MULTIPLICATION** OF THE GOSPEL.
>
> SESSION 3 IS ABOUT
> THE **LANGUAGE** OF THE GOSPEL.
>
> SESSION 4 IS ABOUT
> THE **BEHAVIOUR** OF THE GOSPEL.
>
> SESSION 5 IS ABOUT
> **COMMITTING** TO MULTIPLYING THE GOSPEL.

NOTES

Session 1
The Value of the Gospel

Watch Big Idea
VIDEOS.EXPONENTIAL.EU

Watch Session 1
VIDEOS.EXPONENTIAL.EU

ØYSTEIN GJERME

Øystein Gjerme is the visionary leader of Exponential Europe. He is also the founder and lead pastor of Salt Bergen Church in Norway and the head of the Norwegian Pentecostal movement. He has a Master of Divinity and was chairman of the Norwegian School of Leadership and Theology. For many years he led the multi-denominational movement Sendt Norway, whose primary purpose is to help church planting. Øystein is a speaker and lecturer in many different contexts and has written several books. He is married to Gina, and together they have three children.

Questions

1. What does the gospel mean to you?
2. How is the gospel Good News to the people around you?
3. How did you come to faith? Use some time to share you story in 1-3 minutes.

NOTES

NOTES

NOTES

Session 2
The Value of Multiplication of the Gospel

Watch Session 2
VIDEOS.EXPONENTIAL.EU

RAPHAEL ANZENBERGER

Raphael studied at the University Louis Pasteur, Strasbourg, and Columbia International University, USA. He owns a M.Sc., M.Div, a D.Min, and a Ph.D. He is the President of France Evangelisation, the co-founder of the Global Evangelist Forum, the co-founder of the European Think-Tank on the National Church Planting Processes, a scholar in residence for the Lausanne Church Planting Issue Group, adjunct professor of intercultural Studies (CIU, FLTE), the president of imagoDei and the General Secretary of the French-speaking Baptist Union of Canada. Furthermore, he received the Sandy Ford Scholarship in 2001 and the Billy Graham Lausanne Scholarship in 2018. He is a consultant and speaker with Exponential Europe. He is also the author and co-author of several books, including *(re) Discovering the ministry of the evangelist*. He is married to Karen and they have four kids.

Questions

1. Raphael uses a concept from Jerry Gillis:

    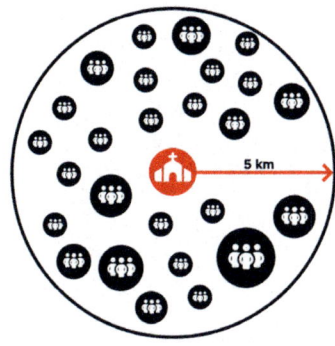

    a. What is the circle of responsibility of you and your church?

    b. Do the people in your neighborhood have access to the gospel? If yes, how?

    c. How can you contribute to the accessibility of the gospel in your circle of responsibility?

2. Do you share the seed generously? If yes, how? If not, why not?

3. Have you experienced the gospel falling on fertile soil and producing fruit? Share the story.

NOTES

NOTES

NOTES

Session 3
The Language of the Gospel

Watch Session 3
VIDEOS.EXPONENTIAL.EU

EMMA BERGKVIST

Emma is Alpha Youth Sweden Director and is passionate about creating opportunities for young people to explore faith. She has been working with youth and encouraging them to share their faith since she was a teenager herself, mainly through a Christian school organization, New Generation, in which students organize themselves to share faith in schools and universities in a very natural and everyday life kind of way. Emma is a speaker and wants to raise the conversation about Gen Z and how we can lead, support and reach the young generation with the gospel. She has written a book for teenagers about taking their first steps in leadership.

Questions

1. What small initiative can I take today at my workplace, at my university or in my local community that God can multiply?

2. What people do I meet in my everyday life that I can invite to my church, Alpha or just to my home?

3. How can I become more confident in sharing my own testimony?

4. If following Jesus means ending up with people, what does that mean in my life?

5. What can I start praying about that will help me focus more on the not yet believers in my life?

NOTES

NOTES

NOTES

Session 4
The Behaviour of the Gospel

Watch Session 4
VIDEOS.EXPONENTIAL.EU

WORKSHOP SESSION

In this session, we will explore various perspectives on the behaviour of the gospel through a set of videos provided by our partners. Scan the QR code above to access the videos and choose one of them. As you watch, take note of key points and ideas that resonate with you, and use the space provided in this workbook to jot down your thoughts and reflections. We want to give you some time for discussion after watching the video with the goal of creating a deeper appreciation of the gospel's impact and inspire meaningful conversation among all participants.

NOTES

NOTES

NOTES

Session 5
Commitment to Multiplying the Gospel

Watch Session 5
VIDEOS.EXPONENTIAL.EU

VLAD CRIZNIC

Vlad is a Regional Leader for Exponential Europe. He graduated from the Emanuel University of Oradea, majoring in Theology, and later on studied at the King's College London for his M.A and PhD. For more than 15 years, Vlad has led the apologetics movement through the RZIM/Think Ask Ponder Romania. He is actively involved in debates, interviews, and conferences, both in Romania and other Romanian Christian communities worldwide, and has written and edited several books, including *Apologetica in Jurul Mesei* (Eng: *A roundtable Apologetics Discussion*) and *(i)Relevant Christian(ity)*. Together with his wife, Dora, and their four children, Vlad lives in Cluj, Romania, where he is one of three pastors of 'Via' Church.

Questions

1. It is our responsibility to sow the seed. What are you doing already and what do you want to change to do this?

2. Do you have a preferred way to share the gospel?

3. What is challenging for you when it comes to sharing the gospel? Share your challenges with each other. Then, pray for each other and bless each other.

NOTES

NOTES

NOTES

Next Steps
An invitation to reflect and to ask God: 'What are You telling me?'

Take some time to reflect on everything you heard during this Roundtable. Use the note section below.

» What resonated with you?
» What challenged you?

Write down three action steps you want to take.

How are you making yourself accountable for implementing those action steps?

Sharing and praying:
» Share your notes around your table.
» Pray for each other and bless each other.

NOTES

I want to take action

Roundtables create an environment where you sit around tables with people from your city, to dream about multiplication of the Gospel.

Start one in your city now!

EXURL.EU/RT

Support us
Give what this is worth to you

This workbook
is offered to you
for free. We want
to continue in
this way, and you
can support it.

Scan to give

EXURL.EU/GIVE

What we Offer

Exponential Europe offers several possibilities to stay connected with other church leaders and planters:

LEADERSHIP CONFERENCE

Every other year, Exponential Europe offers a pan-European Leadership Conference on a topic related to church planting. This conference creates a conversation about a topic related to reproduction and multiplication in a non-denominational setting. We share, learn from each other and create possibilities of collaboration. Do not miss it. Check our website and register to receive our Newsletter:

exponential.eu

ROUNDTABLES

Roundtables create an environment where you sit together around tables with other people from your city, listen to teachings, discuss what you have heard and learn from each other. Use this Workbook in your church, house group or leadership team.

exponential.eu/roundtables

REGIONALS

Regionals are conferences in your language in your region. Meet other leaders, get inspired, encouraged, and equipped. Check our website where and when we offer the next Exponential Regional in your country:

exponential.eu/regionals

Going Deeper
About the authors

City to City Europe focuses on church planting for the renewal of the cities in Europe and content resources for leaders who want to bring the power of the Gospel to every part of life. We seek to catalyze and serve a Europe-wide movement of leaders who create new churches, new ventures, and new expressions of the gospel of Jesus Christ for the common good. We do this by: raising Leaders, platning Churches, and developing City Networks.

City to City Europe is birthed from Redeemer City to City in New York and has been steadily growing to serve the cities in Europe by raising local leaders. We help recruit, train, coach and fund national church planters from a variety of denominational backgrounds in over 30 cities in Europe. We are now seeing these networks multiply churches, become self-sustaining and advance the Gospel in their cities.

TIM COOMAR

ALEXANDER DEUSCHER

STEPHAN PUES

NEIL POWELL

TIM COOMAR

Tim is currently the Interim Director of City to City Europe. He grew up in the UK but has been living in Greece for the past 16 years. In 2011, he planted a church in downtown Athens, where he still lives. Tim is married to Cynthia and they have three children.

ALEXANDER DEUSCHER

Alexander spent the last 10 years planting and leading a church based in Berlin-Friedrichshain called Projekt:Kirche. He recently handed over the church's leadership to his successor and now does Spiritual Formation work for local Berliners and European church planters. He is also on staff at Europe Collaboration, an initiative to support church planting efforts in Europe's city centers. Alex and his wife, Shannon, are enjoying life in the city with their two young boys.

STEPHAN PUES

Stephan is the director of City To City Europe with the vision to create movements of the gospel in the cities of Europe. He was born in Germany, studied at the free theological seminary in Gießen and was a youth-pastor. In 2009 he moved to Frankfurt to plant a church. Together with other leaders he started the center for church planting in Frankfurt. Stephan is married to Verena and they have 3 young children. Together they planted a church in Frankfurt. In his free time he does downhill biking, he draws, he plays with legos and he loves to travel the cities.

NEIL POWELL

Neil is Director of The London Project and also works for City to City Europe. He came to faith as a student in London and got married to his wife Jane here. He divides his time between London and Birmingham. He has a heart to see churches from different tribes working together to serve the city for the gospel and has written about it in his book *Together For The City*. He is excited by the opportunity to learn from existing churches, serve them, enable them to grow and to plant new churches across London.

What is the Gospel?
By Tim Coomar

A life-giving message

The gospel is the message, contained in the whole Bible, about the good news of Jesus Christ, the Son of God. Before we get into the content of the gospel and break down this statement, we must first emphasise what 'kind' of message it is. It is the whole of the message that tells us what that truly *is*.

Madeleine L'Engle is most illuminating on this point. She writes:

> *We draw people to Christ not by loudly discrediting what they believe, by telling them how wrong they are and how right we are, but by showing them a light that is so lovely that they want with all their hearts to know the source of it.[1]*

The gospel is, quite simply, the most wonderful beauty this world has known, and will ever know. For it reintroduces us to God in all his glory, after we had turned our backs on him. As such, God's beauty is revealed in his mercy; his glory is seen in his grace, as he reached out to us and worked our salvation while we were still sinners. As our friend Tim Keller used to say on repeat until we got it, the gospel is the message that I am so sinful that the Son of God himself had to die for me, but at the same time so loved and accepted that he gladly chose to die for me.

There is no glory that compares to this; when truly seen and grasped in the gospel, the God we encounter in Jesus captivates us so utterly that we cannot bear to take our eyes off him. His beauty reanimates us; it is light and healing and life from the dead. Just like the Israelites in the desert when they looked upon the bronze serpent, it is only as we gaze upon the Son of Man lifted up in humiliation and glory that we finally receive life and are made whole ourselves (John 3:14-15).

So the gospel is not just a message; it is a life-giving message. It is not just a story; it is the story of stories. This is why, for us to answer the question, *What is the gospel?*, we must begin with the heart. We must approach the gospel not as an exam we are supposed to study for and sit, but as a song we are supposed to listen to, which draws us to its source, the very life of God, given for us. It is only when someone begins to see and experience the gospel as the beauty of

---
1 Madeleine L'Engle, Walking on Water

God, that they have begun to understand it truly. For that is when its power enters their hearts and they pass from death to life.

One day, when Jesus was teaching, many of those who had been following him turned away upon hearing his claim that he is the bread of life, which has come down from heaven. Simon Peter, however, takes us to the heart of what the gospel is when he responds in that moment: *'Lord, to whom shall we go? You have the words of eternal life'* (John 6:68 (CSB)). Peter had glimpsed the beauty, and could no longer deny its life-giving majesty. This is what the apostle Paul means when he writes in Romans 1:16 that the gospel **is** the power of God for salvation for all who believe.

A story to be (re)told

Of course, none of this denies that the gospel is indeed a story that one can learn and even retell. This is, after all, what evangelism is all about. In contrast to mystery religions, which offer arcane power only to an initiated few, or civic religions, which establish an elite hierarchy, Christianity offers the very power of God to all who draw near to hear and confess the simple – even foolish – message of Christ crucified and raised from the dead.

Moreover, the gospel is a story with a particular interpretation. We are not free to take the facts and events of the gospel story and apply them to our lives however we please; rather, the meaning is already laid out for us in the words of Scripture. It is this already-existing interpretation that constrains and transforms our understanding, not only of the gospel but of reality and life in its entirety, since the gospel message encompasses and affects everything.

This message, contained in the Bible, states that Jesus of Nazareth is the same person as the Word who was always with God and who is himself God, one with and loved by the Father from all eternity. As the eternal Son, he took on flesh, according to the Scriptures, to become for us the Messiah of God, the promised King who will sit on David's throne to establish an everlasting kingdom of righteousness on the earth. It also tells us that he died for our sins, the one righteous human in place of the many unrighteous, according to the Scriptures. Finally, it declares that he arose bodily to indestructible new life in the power of the Holy Spirit, according to the Scriptures, and is thus the first fruit of the new creation, the beginning of the promised shalom of God finally filling the earth when he returns to rule. Thus the resurrection is truly and ultimately the answer to every deep hope of humanity, both for itself and for the world. It is *'dignity spread over the cosmos like a blanket'*[2]

---

2 Cole Arthur Riley, This Here Flesh, p8

These are the truths contained in the Bible and articulated in the historic creeds of Christianity, and while they are by no means the full account of the gospel, they do represent the irreducible minimum core of the gospel (incarnation, substitution, resurrection) without which its power is nullified. There is only one gospel.

A God who speaks your language

At the same time, what we also observe is that this one gospel comes to us in many, varied forms. Not only is it multi-faceted and all-encompassing, covering the whole scope of existence and history, from creation, to fall, to redemption, it is also polyphonic, effectively communicating these truths to any and every tribe, nation, and culture. Indeed, it is precisely its multifaceted nature that allows it to be so polyphonic and transhistorical, as different cultures throughout history are able to connect to different points or forms of the story, and so encounter the whole by coming to it via different entry points.

One of the clearest examples of this in the New Testament is found in the distinction between the 'gospel to the circumcised' and the 'gospel to the uncircumcised', referring to how the gospel was communicated by the apostles to Jewish and non-Jewish audiences respectively[3]. It is clear from these varied presentations of the gospel that different aspects or forms of the one gospel story may be emphasised depending on the audience. To the Jews, Peter proclaims Jesus as the fulfilment of the Law and the Prophets, and the rightful heir of David's throne, with attestation of his identity and power through miracles, signs, and wonders. To the Gentiles Paul proclaims Jesus as the creator God, the Logic of the universe, to whom they are already feeling their way in the dark, albeit at his own prompting, but to whom they must now turn in repentance in light of the resurrection.

In 1 Corinthians, this idea is expounded further, as Paul explains how the cross offends people from different cultures in different ways, depending on what their most prominent idols are. For the Greeks, who seek wisdom, the cross is foolishness, since it portrays a God who lowers himself to bring about his purposes through an apparently nonsensical sacrifice. For the Jews, who seek power, the cross is scandalous, since it accomplishes redemption through the weakness and abominable shame of a gentile cross. In both cases, however, the wisdom and power that these groups of people seek are ultimately to be found in the cross, only in a subverted form. The gospel is, therefore, the answer

---
3 Cf. Gal 2:7-9

to the heartfelt cry not only of humanity in a general sense but more specifically and tangibly of every culture throughout history. When communicated effectively and in the appropriate form, it resonates with the human heart in ways that other cultural narratives can only ever, at best, yearn for or echo.

The way back to ourselves

The church has often implicitly communicated that affirming the truth of the gospel merely at the level of intellectual assent is sufficient to tap into its power. This is to misunderstand what the gospel is. The purpose of hearing and receiving the gospel is to be personally reintroduced to the God who created us, to be united with him in Christ, and to find ourselves in him. Our hearts must be involved in the process of both apprehending and confessing the truth about Jesus. Paul writes to the Romans:

> *That is the message concerning faith that we proclaim: If you declare with your mouth, 'Jesus is Lord,' and believe in your heart that God raised him from the dead, you will be saved.*
>
> Rom 10:8-9 (CSB)

The gospel is not only intellectually true, it is existentially satisfying. When we truly believe the gospel, we are led from a place of being lost to being found, from being orphans to being adopted by God, from being enemies of God to sitting at his table as his friends. This is what Jesus' disciples experienced directly with him, and what today we may also experience through the Holy Spirit who calls us to sit at the Lord's table each week to enjoy fellowship together with the God who created us, loved us, and gave himself for us. John Calvin sums it up, saying,

> *...indeed it is vain for any to philosophize in the manner of the world, unless they have first been humbled by the preaching of the gospel, and have instructed the whole compass of their intellect to submit to the foolishness of the cross... Nothing further can be done, if we are not raised up from the lowest depths and carried aboard his cross above all the heavens, so that there by faith we might comprehend what no eye has ever seen, nor ear ever heard, and which far surpasses our hearts and minds. For the earth is not before us there, nor its fruits supplied for daily food, but Christ himself offers himself to us unto eternal life.*[4]

---

4 John Calvin, Commentary on the Book of Genesis

What is the Gospel? It is the Word from God, who makes sense of God by bringing the reality of God into our hearts and lives, so that we may live again, truly. As the Psalmist proclaims, *'Blessed are those who dwell in your house, they are ever praising you'* (Psalms 84:4 (CSB)).

NOTES

NOTES

Witnessing the Power of the Gospel

By Alexander Deuscher

An Astounding Disconnect

At the beginning of *2001 – A Space Odyssey*, a black box falls from the sky, mysterious and unknowable, yet so massive and unmissable that it becomes a disturbance in the landscape, an irritation in everyone's life, a looming question right at the heart of civilization.

If we dare to admit it, most Christian leaders in Europe experience a similar situation: We also have a massive **thing** sitting right in our otherwise neatly ordered understanding of reality, putting everything we believe into question. It is a black box, puzzling, disorienting, and frankly, quite challenging to engage with. Still, it is there, and it is this: there is an astounding disconnect between the beauty of the gospel and the current spiritual landscape in Europe! On one hand, we see 'the most beautiful thing known to man,' which, by all means, should captivate everyone's attention. On the other hand, however, we experience an utter disinterest and indifference towards this message that seems to keep growing at a rapid rate. Some of us have gotten so used to this disconnect that we barely notice it anymore, but if we dare to look again, this **thing** is mind-boggling, really! And it begs the question: what is going on? What can we do to change it?

Naturally, in search of an answer, our instincts lead us to evangelism first: better apologetics, cutting-edge outreach events, and training people to share the gospel – let's pray, preach, go out, and save the lost! This impulse is certainly valid, but in focusing on what we might be doing, we tend to overlook a very crucial piece of the puzzle: which is the *people* who are doing the praying, the preaching, and saving the lost – **us!** – because the message is never separated from its messengers. Yes, the gospel in and of itself is incredibly beautiful for those who see it, but to a non-believing (and thus not-looking-at-it) world, its beauty becomes visible and accessible in what it accomplishes in us.

In other words: One key to solving this mystery and seeing Europe marvel at the beauty of the gospel (once again) might not be better strategies or fire-hot prayer meetings (though both have their importance), but letting the gospel by the power of the Holy Spirit do what it/He does best: transforming broken human beings into still broken, yet incredibly *beautiful* human beings. The best way to evangelise might be to apply the gospel over and over again to our own hearts, and let our surroundings see in real time 'what it can do'! Or, to go back to *2001* once again: it is we Christians who could become the black box, disturbing the otherwise neatly ordered (inner) landscape of Europeans, becoming this looming question right at the heart of civilization – what or who is creating such strangely beautiful humans?

Paul and Berlin

Now for some of us, this might be a strange way to think about evangelism. But for Paul, it probably was one of the essential ways to evangelise and disciple others. In our reading of his letters, it can be challenging sometimes to notice how often he talks about himself. At one point, he goes so far as to say we should *'follow my example, as I follow the example of Christ'* (1 Cor 11:1). This can easily strike us as arrogant – who does he think he is, that we would want to imitate him? Yet what Paul was doing here and in other places, was simply to invite the people around him to have a closer look at him and who he was becoming through the power of the gospel! He was confident enough to think that people would look at him and say: *'Oh man, I want what he has ... because I would really like to be more like **him**!'* For Paul, it is important what we ***do***, but it is even more important who we ***are*** (or are becoming). In other words: the most important thing we have to offer to an unbelieving Europe is, as Ruth Haley Barton puts it, our *'transforming selves'*![5]

Are you a person worth following? Do people look at us and say: *'I want to be like **her**.'* This warmth, this loving honesty, the unhurried way she is present with me in a conversation, his ability to admit when he is wrong, how much she's okay with not having an answer, not needing to fix things – I want that. At least in my experience (of church planting in Berlin for over 10 years), Europeans will not respond (as much) to tracts on the street or fiery sermons from the pulpit, but they do respond to people they're drawn to because they feel *safe*. They start getting curious when they sense that someone is a Christian, yet familiar with dark nights of the soul. They respond to people who are dealing with their deepest wounds and are transparent about it. The *best* thing we have to offer (to an unbelieving Europe) is our being-transformed-by-the-gospel self!

---

5 Ruth Haley Barton, Strengthening the Soul of Your Leadership: Seeking God in the Crucible of Ministry

But how does the gospel bring such change? And how can we experience it? Let's have a closer look.

The Power of the Gospel and Facing our Shadows

Tim Keller applies the gospel to each of us in this way:

> *The Christian Gospel is that I am so flawed that Jesus had to die for me, yet I am so loved and valued that Jesus was glad to die for me.*[6]

We are more flawed than we ever dared believe **and** more loved than we ever dared hope. Our brokenness is even bigger than we imagined **and** God is even crazier about us than we thought possible. There are many ways in which we could apply this incredible message to our hearts, but when it comes down to it, God invites us through the gospel to simply be *human* again: to have an honest look at ourselves and see the utterly beautiful as well as the depth of our brokenness, and then allow God to love *us as who we are*.

Now this is much harder than it sounds. Our temptation will always be to either not dare to look at our brokenness as closely, or to not allow God to love *us as we are*. Both, however, are ways in which we resist the transformational power of the gospel – so let's have a closer look.

On one hand, some of us are quick to jump to the comfort of a loving God who 'accepts me just the way I am'. No need for introspection. No need to second-guess myself. Criticism gets brushed off quickly as a power move, as unfair, or simply as an 'indication that I'm a sinner who needs grace.' There is an unwillingness to face what Pete Scazzero calls 'our shadow':

> *Your shadow is the accumulation of untamed emotions, less-than-pure motives and thoughts that, while largely ignored, strongly influence and shape your behaviours. It is the damaged but mostly hidden version of who you are.*[7]

This shadow can come out in all sorts of ways – through attempts to control others, outbursts of anger, bitterness, or escapism, just as much as through a need to rescue others, to always be noticed, or an unhealthy drive to always be working. While it may be much easier to ignore our shadow and 'rest in the fact that God loves us *as we are*', it doesn't produce the attractiveness of character that Paul believes will draw

---

6 Tim Keller, The Reason for God: Belief in an Age of Skepticism

7 Pete Scazzero, The Emotionally Healthy Leader: How Transforming Your Inner Life will Deeply Transform your Church, Team, and the World

people to the gospel. It's quite the opposite, really: ignoring our shadows will simply create constant unrest in our hearts, which makes it sometimes exciting, but eventually exhausting and unsafe to be around us. We might be unaware of it, but there's an inner drivenness that we can't quite shake. Silence and solitude become uncomfortable quickly, and so we always need to distract ourselves with work, ministry, meeting lots of people, and pulling out our devices in every free moment. Eventually, this inner unrest sets us on a path for some crisis moment, be it burnout, moral failure, or starting to be harmful (rather than helpful) to the people we serve and lead. There is this deep inner work that God wants to (and needs to) do in us, but we struggle to open ourselves up to him this way.

What is really underneath all of this, of course, oftentimes isn't an overly strong confidence, but the opposite, it's a deep insecurity. Through certain experiences in childhood and adulthood, a deep belief might have been formed in us that really, we are not 'enough' – which will then lead us to either overcompensate by making ourselves 'bigger' than we actually are (and not daring to look at our shadow side), or on the other hand, making ourselves 'smaller': Our self-confidence is shaky to begin with, so every failure in life becomes another proof of our unworthiness, every criticism utterly crushes us, and 'Jesus loves you so much, he died for you' in the end just feels like a reminder that we are so bad, it cost God his life! So really, how dare we?

And while we might try to clothe this deep-sitting insecurity as humility, it really isn't – as CS Lewis has pointed out, *'humility is not thinking less of yourself, it's thinking of yourself less'*.[8] And this deep insecurity will also bleed into every aspect of our life and ministry. We might constantly try to please everybody, struggle to stand up for what we believe or attach in unhealthy ways to 'stronger' personalities around us. If unaddressed, this also doesn't produce the attractiveness of character that Paul believes will draw people to the gospel.

So, how does the power of the gospel start to grab a hold of us then? I believe there are two aspects of life in which we can start to apply it to ourselves and allow the Spirit to do His transformative work: to us, and to our community.

The Power of the Gospel in Me

John Calvin opens his Magnum Opus, the *Institutes*, in this way:

---

[8] This actual quote is from Rick Warren, *The Purpose Driven Life: What on Earth Am I Here For?*, who summarised a thought developed by CS Lewis in Mere Christianity.

Without knowledge of self, there is no knowledge of God.[9]

Allowing the gospel to truly grasp and transform us (and thus knowing and experiencing God) will always start with 'knowledge of self', an unflinching look in the mirror. Yes, we live by grace alone, and yes, we have accepted Jesus as our Lord and Saviour, but in our everyday lives, it oftentimes isn't God's grace that gives us a sense of worth and identity, but our successes or failures, our place in the world (or in the church); and similarly, it oftentimes isn't Jesus in whom we trust to be in control and *'save'* us, but we look to money, power, love or other *'saviours'* to give us security or control. Becoming aware of what is really going on in our hearts – as sobering as it might be – is nothing other than an invitation for God's Spirit to continue His work in us, slowly but surely helping us to live out of God's love on a much deeper level.

This awareness will not come naturally, however. We need to find times to not just sit with God's word, but sit with our own hearts. It is where God will meet us and transform us.

The Power of the Gospel in Community

In my experience, Christian community can oftentimes be a very lonely place. Dietrich Bonhoeffer writes:

The pious fellowship permits no one to be a sinner. So everybody must conceal his sin from himself and from the fellowship. We dare not be sinners. Many Christians are unthinkably horrified when a real sinner is suddenly discovered among the righteous. So we remain alone with our sin, living in lies and hypocrisy.[10]

This is what happens when we don't allow the gospel to shape our community: It becomes a lonely place, a place of pretending, coercion, and deeply unsafe. The power of the gospel, however, is that it puts us on 'eye level' with each other – we are both much worse than we thought (and thus capable of even the biggest sins), but we are also much more loved than we ever dared to hope (and thus incredibly precious and beautiful in God's sight). In theory, this great equaliser will make for a powerful community.

Again, however, this kind of community does not come naturally. It will take applying the gospel radically both to how I see myself and how I see you: I am neither better (and

---

9 John Calvin, Institutes of the Christian Religion

10 Dietrich Bonhoeffer, Life Together

thus bigger) than you, nor will I allow you to make me smaller. I will not be surprised by your weaknesses or sinful behaviours, but also learn to appreciate your strengths without being too impressed by it. We meet on eye level. And, we need to learn to become vulnerable with each other and share both our struggles and our victories, and experience true community through the gospel.

NOTES

NOTES

Multiplying the gospel
By Stephan Pues

The good old gospel. The greatest, most beautiful, most powerful, best message in the world. The good news from the cross of Jesus Christ. This gospel has over the centuries reached the whole world, touched and changed billions of lives, and is still one of the most shared and loved truths in the world today. It seems to be part of the nature of the gospel that it wants to be shared and spread. It is like a seed of a plant that seeks to grow and naturally multiply. Gospel multiplication.

The previous chapters showed what the gospel is and how it changes us. In this chapter, one of the most significant aspects of the gospel is discussed. The multiplication aspect of the gospel. Often this is called evangelism.

In Genesis 1 it is described how God created the world. In verses 11-12 the story of the third day is told:

> Then God said, 'Let the land produce vegetation: seed-bearing plants and trees on the land that bear fruit with seed in it, according to their various kinds.' And it was so. The land produced vegetation: plants bearing seed according to their kinds and trees bearing fruit with seed in it according to their kinds. And God saw that it was good.
>
> Gen 1:11-12

This day was a great day of creation. Some of the greatest things saw the light for the first time: trees, flowers, cacti, vegetables, and fruits. And they came with a fundamental godly principle that is described in the verses: They had seeds. And those seeds were made for multiplication. The plants had seeds and in the seed was the potential to fill the whole world by multiplication. Not addition or recreation is the principle, but multiplication. This principle and picture will guide us in thinking about spreading the gospel in our world today.

It is maybe one of the most crucial and critical questions of the church in Europe in the 21st century: Evangelism? Sharing the gospel with others? Is that something we should still do? Haven't we overcome this? Isn't that something for very gifted or professional Christians? How can we make it work? What if the people don't like it? In a post-Christian time where many people

in Europe don't think very highly about the church and its faith, we need to think well about the question of evangelism.

Why?

In Mark 4 we find Jesus talking to his disciples and the crowd around him. He is explaining principles of the Kingdom of God. He uses an example twice: A farmer scatters seed on his farmland. In verses 1 to 20 the story includes that some of the seeds are fruitful because they fall on fertile ground and others are not, because of obstacles. The second time he uses the example is in verses 26 to 29. There the focus is more on the long process it takes for the seeds to grow and bear fruit. The growth of the seeds is not dependent on anything the farmer does. The power is in the seed. If things go right, it will grow. And it takes time. It is just a tiny little seed, but it has the potential to be a big plant. That is how the gospel is. It has power. We don't need to add power to it.

In both cases, Jesus uses this comic-style story to explain to the people around him one of the fundamental principles in the Kingdom of God: that the word, the message, the gospel is scattered. The good news is shared and spread out. That is what happens if things are going right. It is not even an option. It happens naturally. The farmer doesn't wait or consider if he has to or wants to do it. He does it, because it is normal. In the Kingdom of God, the sharing of the gospel is as natural as a fish that swims or a light that shines. Even though the results are insecure and predictably diverse, the farmer still does what he always does, he scatters. Our job is to be witnesses of Jesus and his gospel. We are called to sow, not to grow the plant.

After Jesus' death and resurrection, he instructed his followers to do what he told them in parables: To bring the gospel to everyone in the world. And that is what then happened after he went back to heaven. The church started sharing the gospel like crazy. They did what Jesus explained in his parables. They acted like a farmer scattering the seeds. And it worked. The growth of the Christian faith and church in the first three centuries is the fastest growth of any religious group in history. It multiplied from 120 people in Acts 2 to half of the population of the Roman Empire three centuries later. They kept doing what was normal in the church: They shared the gospel.

My son's most famous Marvel superhero is Thor. A cool, strong, funny guy who saves the world several times in every movie. He has a slogan, he keeps repeating. Every time he needs to do something challenging and gets asked why he does it, he recites, *'Because that's what heroes do'*. That is what Jesus explains about the Kingdom of God. The gospel is scattered. *'Because*

that's what Christians do'. Sharing the gospel is like what the farmer did: spreading it everywhere. The gospel is not just the beginning of Christian faith, it is all of it. It is not the ABC, but the A-Z.

I think the church in Europe needs to be reminded of this simple posture and relearn this practice, to share the gospel. After many centuries when the vast majority of people in many parts of Europe claimed to be Christians, we are now back to a reality where many people don't believe in the gospel and see the Christian faith and the church critically. Some call this the post-Christian time. As the church of Jesus, we are called especially in this generation to renew this normality. That we act like farmers who scatter the word from the cross, the gospel in our world. Because that is what Christians do.

Who?

The simple idea of multiplication from Genesis 1 implies that everyone who has the gospel is ready to multiply. Like with plants. Every tree, flower, and fruit multiples. Not just a few who are especially gifted or equipped or trained. Everyone who receives and believes the gospel is able to multiply.

Often the idea of every Christian sharing the gospel with others causes fear, pressure, discomfort, or at least insecurity. There were and are many stories of how Christians were almost forced to evangelise others. That can lead to a way of evangelism that feels forceful, irrelevant, or even aggressive. I don't think that is the idea Jesus had. The gospel is the greatest news the world has ever heard. It causes joy and freedom.

This joy and freedom in the gospel helps us to see that we are called, commanded, and competent to share the gospel.

» **We are called:** Because of our calling to be part of God's family we have a new identity. This new identity is to be part of a Kingdom that spreads.

» **We are commanded:** In Matthew 28, Jesus commands his disciples to go to the ends of the earth and spread his gospel. So when we do that we do something the God of the universe actually wants from us. And we can rely on him, blessing and helping us.

» **We are competent:** We know the gospel ourselves. Everyone who believes it has a personal way to explain and share it. It is in this way, through the simple witnesses of all kinds of people, not just professionals, how Jesus wants his gospel to be multiplied. And we have the Holy Spirit in us. Jesus promised that he will help us. So we shouldn't worry too much.

When?

The question of when to share the gospel with someone is very connected to the question of how and what that means. With this question the parable of the farmer does not work so well. Farmers only spread in special seasons. But sharing the gospel is not only to be done in spring, but all the time. Paul writes to his friend Timothy, *'preach the word; be ready in season and out of season'* (2 Tim 4:2). So basically, as often as possible. We need a relaxed balance between too much pressure to perform maximum evangelism and a shy or unintentional silence. Some people push too hard; many others are too silent. The simple idea is to apply the gospel to everyone and everything all the time and find ways to be a witness of Jesus and what he has done. This is how the gospel spreads.

Where?

Most people in Europe, when they think about the place where they need to go to hear the gospel, probably think about a church building. And that is probably a good place to go. In the church, in its songs, its programs, its sermons, and its groups you should find and hear the gospel. In reality, sadly that is not always the case, but that is a good place to go. A growing group of people in Europe don't go to church anymore. So if the idea of Romans 10 *'how are they to hear without someone preaching?'* is still true today, the question of where the gospel is multiplied needs to be considered.

The idea of multiplication is that the farmer goes out to spread the seed. In another parable of Jesus in Luke 15, the idea of going out is even more pushed. He describes the Kingdom of God as a shepherd who has 100 sheep and one gets lost. The shepherd leaves the 99 behind, and goes out in order to seek, find, and bring home the lost one. This is a picture for the church. We are called to go out, not to stay inside and wait for others to come to us. In the same way, the sharing of the gospel should not just happen in the church, but everywhere. Everywhere, where a believer of the gospel is present, the gospel can be spread. In homes, at work, in a cafe, in the gym, in a chatroom, on vacation, in the train etc.

A friend of mine who planted a church shared with me that one of the members of his church is an astronaut who actually went to the ISS (International Space Station). He showed me a picture of his friend watching his sermon on a tablet there. And he had the opportunity to talk to his colleagues about it. So the gospel is to be shared everywhere, in every place, even in space.

If we want to build churches according to the multiplication idea of Jesus, we need to build sending churches. Churches that are communities of people who love, celebrate, and multiply the gospel among them and who are also intentional in taking the gospel everywhere, looking for opportunities to give witness and to do the farmers' work of spreading the gospel. The Church should encourage and equip believers to do that. It is of course a good tradition and posture to invite people to church so that they can hear the gospel there. But not only there.

How?

Now we come to a question that is maybe less important than we may think. Yes, it is good and helpful to ask how we can share the gospel. It is absolutely helpful to grow in competency and knowledge about the gospel and a relevant way to share it. But it can also be over-engineered and explained. I don't need to become a super-expert before I can do it. Sharing the gospel is simple. Everyone can do it. And God can use even the weakest attempt to change people's hearts.

The gospel is the message that we share and it has the power within itself to grow. The gospel is also the principle of how we can share it. In John 20:21 Jesus says to his followers: *'How the Father has sent me I am sending you'*. The way he was sent by his father was by becoming human. He didn't just show up in the sky for ten minutes, gave his message and left. He lived among us. He spent time learning the language, the jokes, the culture, a job, and everything it means to be a human. This is how Jesus is sending us.

When we share the gospel, it is important to share the gospel so that people will understand it and in the best case even believe it. So how can we do that well?

I see five helpful principles on how to share the gospel:

Joyful

A person who has experienced the impact of the gospel as a saving, freeing, meaningful change in life will as a result see many effects. The most immediate and obvious is joy. Because of what Jesus has done for you and what that means for your present and future is so overwhelmingly great, that you will be joyful. And this joy will be the motivation when Christians share their faith. The gospel is not only a truth, but it is the most beautiful truth. Humans are created to react to beauty with affection, amazement, and joy. The reformer Calvin has put it this way:

> *It therefore becomes us also diligently to prosecute that investigation of*

God which so enraptures the soul with admiration as, at the same time, to make an efficacious impression on it.[11]

The beautiful truth of the gospel is so great, that it will cause joy. That joy from the gospel is the best motivation for evangelism. Because of what Jesus has done for me I joyfully want to share that with others.

So if we as individuals or as a church or church plant try to share the gospel with others in our city, let us do it joyfully. The sign is that there is an excitement or a passion behind it. We don't need to be forced to do it. We love to do it. It's a joy.

Brave

The gospel should make us brave in the way we share it. Yes, there are fears, insecurities, and doubts, but the gospel itself is the message, that despite these things we are welcome and included in God's family. So the church is not a community of the ones who were fearless, strong, smart, and secure enough to believe in God. Faith is a gift from God to us, regardless of all reasons that could hold us back. The truth that the almighty God is willing to work through us to invite others to believe in His son and His gospel should make us brave. Because it is not our smartness, our strength, or our security, but Him, that matters. He has even given us His Holy Spirit as an internal superpower that is active when we share the gospel. Paul says, *'I am not ashamed of the gospel, because it is the power of God that brings salvation to everyone who believes'* (Rom 1:16).

So if we share the gospel with everyone around us, we can be brave, because the power of the Spirit, the power of the gospel are in us. No need to fear or hesitate. Let's be brave!

Clear

Because of the nature of the gospel, to be a message, the message must be clear and correct. Remembering as a kid, I have often had to play the game Chinese whispers. One starts with a message and it is passed to others and because of misunderstanding or kids that want to be funny, the message gets changed on the way. There is a danger that this happens to the gospel too. Paul in the letter to the Galatians is unusually strict when it comes to this. He is very eager to ensure that the message of the gospel stays clear. We need to protect it and ensure it is not foggy, incorrect, watered down, or compromised. The gospel only has power if it is correct. Church history has proven that if the gospel is changed, the church loses its power and significance. It is important to have the gospel straight, clear, and deep.

---

11 The Institutes Of The Christian Religion, Books First and Second. N.p., Jazzybee Verlag.

So if we share the gospel with others let us make sure that we have a clear and rich understanding of the gospel and that we share it in an uncompromised and full way. If we do that the gospel will challenge and confront people with the beautiful truth of God. It will sometimes not be understood or welcomed – that happened to Jesus too – but only this way will it unfold the power to change people. So let us be clear.

Relevant

Because of the way the gospel has come to us, we are called to share it in a certain way. The gospel came into our world through Jesus, the son of God who from eternity was with his Father in Heaven, who then incarnated. He became human and lived the life we should have lived and died the death we should have died. Then, after he did all the great things that are summarised in the gospel, he said to his disciples, *'How the Father has sent me I am sending you'* (John 20:21). In this statement he says how we are called to share the gospel: in an incarnated way. That means we need to adapt the gospel to the context we are in. Paul practised this very successfully and then explained that he had adopted himself and his gospel-presentation to many different groups: The Jewish, the Greek, the weak. He claims, *'I have become all things to all people so that by all possible means I might save some'* (1 Cor 9:22). He was very good at adapting himself and the way he shared the gospel (not the gospel itself!!!) to the context. Sometimes this process is called contextualisation. It is not meant to say that this changes the gospel itself but it takes into account that there is a culture, a language, a humour, a history, and other things in place that the message of the gospel needs to be contextualised to. The same gospel needs to be shared differently in different ages, languages, cultures, neighbourhoods, and groups. If we do that well, we will be relevant. This is what Jesus calls us to.

So if we share the gospel with others in our generation, our place, our culture, and our personal way, we are called to be relevant. We are called to contextualise it and adapt it to the people we are talking to. Only then will they hear it and hopefully believe it. That's why it is worth it. So let us be relevant.

Humble

The gospel has many results in our lives. One that is very important in the way we share the gospel is humility. Because the gospel is a power of God and it includes the truth that a supernatural miracle is needed to understand and believe it, we should know that we can not produce the response ourselves. Neither the person who shared the gospel nor the one who hears it has a major influence on the results. Even if we are the best gospel communicators or the smartest listeners, we have no influence on how likely the gospel will have an impact or not. It is a part of the miracle of God that it is his sovereign grace that needs to take our witness and our minds and do the miracle of faith. Knowing that makes us both relaxed and humble. In the end, we should not boast and say, *'Look, how great am I that I can share the gospel in such a great way'*. The gospel makes us humble and dependent on God. As a result, neither success nor failure will crush us. Both will bring us to the same prayer: Lord, it is all depending on you. And all the glory belongs to you!

So if we share the gospel with others, let us do it in a way that we are totally relying on God. Let us not push or give up. Let us be humble. For the glory of God.

NOTES

NOTES

The Gospel on Display: one Church in the City

By Neil Powell

Gospel transformation and churches in our cities

It takes all types of churches to reach a city. But do we also believe that all types of churches need to work together to do it? And how does the gospel enable and release the power of collaboration?

When Paul urges the Roman church to embrace gospel renewal (Rom 12:1-2), he has in mind something that extends way beyond our personal holiness, life as a local church, or even our witness to the world outside. The theme of gospel transformation continues in chapters 14-15, where he extends the gospel's reach into unexpected areas: the relationship between different congregations within a city.

The Roman house-church

Read through Romans 16, it becomes clear that the Roman church is made up of multiple house church communities. John Stott suggests that Paul greets the leaders of at least five congregations in the city within this chapter. For example, in verse 3, Paul says, *'Greet Pricscilla and Aquila, my co-workers in Christ Jesus'*, and in verse 5, *'Greet also the church that meets at their house'*. Crucially, Paul sees these different gospel communities as all part of the one church of Jesus Christ in the city (Rom 1:7).

The problem with the church in Rome that becomes clear in chapters 14-15 is that the different house churches are not getting along. Despite a shared love for Jesus, their differing views on secondary issues have driven them apart.

Commentators suggest that the *'weak'* and *'strong'* believers in Chapter 14 are essentially Jewish and Gentile communities. The *'weak'* won't eat certain meats and wish to observe special holy days. The *'strong'* disagree and believe that Christians are free to eat all things, and to them, all days are the same.

An important clue to the situation in Rome is that, for several years, all Jews were expelled from the city by decree of the Roman emperor. This included Jewish believers in Jesus. During this period, the church in Rome was entirely Gentile. After the Jewish Christians were allowed to return, it appears they were not welcomed and included by their Gentile brothers and sisters in the church.

Ollerton writes that in chapters 14-15, *'Paul's primary concern is that the house churches don't fragment into ghettos of Jewish and Roman Christians who mistrust one another'.*[12]

What is revealed in Romans, then, are fellowships within the same city that refuse to acknowledge each other and are unwilling to work together, preferring to pass judgement and condemn one another. This is a situation we still witness in our cities around the world.

Richard Longenecker adds, *'The apostle's purpose was to restore peace and unity within the Christian congregations at Rome, and so to enhance an accurate expression of the Christian gospel in the city'.*[13]

What is fascinating about Romans 14-15 is not just that Paul longs to see different fellowships working together in a city as an application of the gospel, but how Paul brings the gospel to bear in his appeal for unity within the church in the city.

---

[12] Ollerton, Andrew. Romans: A Letter That Makes Sense of Life. United Kingdom, John Murray Press, 2023.

[13] Longenecker, Richard N.. The Epistle to the Romans. United Kingdom, Wm. B. Eerdmans Publishing Company, 2016.

It is not unity in uniformity that he seeks, but unity in diversity. And the gospel is the power to bring the church together despite its differences.

Rather than judge or condemn one another (on issues he describes as 'matters of indifference' (Rom 14:1)), Paul puts the unity of God's people as a visible expression of the gospel ahead of doctrinal differences.

He knows whose side he is on in the debate that divides these groups. He celebrates the freedoms the gospel gives to eat all foods, for example, and regards the inability of the weak to accept this as a failing (Rom 15:1). However, crucially, the gospel means that such differences must not divide those whom Jesus Christ has accepted. And he has accepted them – *'weak'* and *'strong'* – just as they are; whether they worship with a tender conscience or a greater freedom, God does not discriminate. The principle Paul wants to establish is that those who are united to Jesus in the gospel should not allow themselves to be divided, even though they practice their faith in different ways based on their different convictions.

In chapters 14-15, the keyword in the argument is the Greek word proslambano. It appears in the opening verse (Rom 14:1) and the closing verse (Rom 15:7). Bookends to the whole. It means most literally 'to take in'. So elsewhere in the Bible, it's used

to describe taking food into our bodies, taking strangers into our home, and here in Romans, it means taking in other believers into our hearts and our lives.

The key verse serves as Paul's climax to his argument, where he writes *'Accept [take into your hearts] one another, as Christ has accepted you'* (Rom 15:7). What the gospel requires - peace and unity between churches in a city - the gospel enables. Why do we love other believers, serve them, work for their flourishing in the city, and go on missions together? We are to accept one another as Christ has accepted us.

Snowflakes and Ice Cubes

In the gospel, we find profound teachings that emphasise the place, value, and importance of diversity. This principle can be beautifully illustrated through the comparison of snowflakes and ice cubes.

When God freezes water, He creates snowflakes, each one being a unique masterpiece of intricate design. No two snowflakes are identical, reflecting the boundless creativity and diversity inherent in God's creation. This natural phenomenon illustrates how diversity is embedded in the very fabric of the universe, as intended by God. We recognize this when we acknowledge different gifts in the church family (1 Cor 12 comes to mind; one body, many parts). What Paul is doing in Romans is arguing that this rich diversity is also seen between congregations and their differences in worship according to conscience. Paul calls on the Christians in Rome to recognise the place of diversity and to see how the gospel upholds and enables diverse Christian groups to love and serve each other.

Unlike God, when we humans freeze water, we make ice cubes—uniform, identical, and predictable. While ice cubes serve their practical purposes, they lack the unique beauty and individuality of snowflakes.

When we decide to co-exist or even compete with other groups of believers in our cities, we not only face missed opportunities for better gospel witnessing, but we actually end up contradicting the gospel with our actions. Paul urges us to live out our faith across denominations and tribes to the glory of God.

So, the gospel not only promotes diversity but enables it too. It promotes diversity in several fundamental ways:

Celebration of Individuality:

» The gospel teaches that every person is a unique creation of God, endowed with individual talents, perspectives,

and experiences. Just as snowflakes reflect the endless creativity of their Creator, each person reflects God's diverse image in their own special way.

Unity in Diversity:

» The gospel calls for unity among believers, not through uniformity but through the harmonious integration of diverse individuals and diverse churches in a city. This mirrors the collective beauty of snowflakes, each contributing its unique design to the vast, stunning landscapes of winter. The church in a city is seen as a body with many parts, each with a distinct role, working together for the common good.

Growth through Varied Perspectives:

» The gospel fosters an environment where diverse ideas and approaches are valued. Just as the diversity of snowflakes adds to the wonder of snowfall, varied perspectives within the church across the city leads to deeper understanding, creativity, and growth. This diversity is not seen as a challenge to unity but as a vital component of it.

Conclusion

Paul uses the gospel to bring churches together in a common mission within a city. As leaders of local churches, we tend to limit our obligations to those who belong to our group and who think exactly as we do. The gospel calls us to take into our hearts other leaders, and the churches they represent even though we disagree on many secondary issues.

In embracing the gospel, believers are encouraged to see the world through the lens of God's creative diversity, much like the unique snowflakes that fall from the sky. We are called to move beyond the uniformity of ice cubes, recognizing and celebrating the unique contributions of each gospel community. In doing so, the gospel not only promotes diversity but also reveals its divine beauty and purpose.

NOTES

NOTES

A Gospel Vision
By Stephan Pues

One of the most encouraging things about the Kingdom of God in Europe for me is how many leaders seem to have and grow a desire to see a movement of the gospel in Europe. I am privileged to travel to many places and meet with leaders in Lisbon, London, Paris, Kyiv, Vienna, Athens, Moscow, and many other places. Even though they are very different, they seem to be inspired and driven by the same hope: We want to see the gospel change us, our churches, and our cities. We feel that God wants to do something on our continent. And that is what we are working towards. Oftentimes with little visible results but big vision and resilience. I see a generation that is dreaming, praying, and acting to see the vision of Jesus growing in Europe. We know that this is a challenging time. But also a time with big opportunities and a time when the gospel is still as beautiful and powerful as always.

In the previous chapters, we discussed what the gospel is, how it affects us, and how we share it with others. Let us now consider how we can be hopeful about the task we have: to be the church multiplying the gospel in our generation.

The vision

Jesus gave his church a vision. He told them, *'you will receive power when the Holy Spirit comes on you; and you will be my witnesses in Jerusalem, and in all Judea and Samaria, and to the ends of the earth'* (Acts 1:8). With his words, he painted a picture of what would happen and what then did happen. A vision of the future: God's spirit will come and as a result, you will witness the gospel of Jesus everywhere. It was not a command. Not an option. Not a wish. It was a vision. The reason why it will come true is that God does it through us. In Matthew 28, in the great commandment, we see the same logic. Jesus says, *'All authority in heaven and on earth has been given to me. Therefore go...'* (Matt 28:18-19). The almighty, sovereign, holding all power and authority, controlling the universe, undefeatable, most glorious, and victorious Jesus, son of the one and only God is the one who gives his church a vision: That we will witness and the result will be a movement of the gospel. People will believe it. Churches will be started. Lives and cities will be changed and this will continue until Jesus comes back.

After Jesus said this, his Father came and took him back to Heaven. But he didn't go there to relax. It is not a vacation on the beach until he is called to come back. He is sitting at the right hand of his Father and is reigning the whole world. He is King. He rules over all nations, all hearts, all authorities, and every individual. He uses his power, his spirit, and his gospel to make the vision he gave to the disciples real: A movement for the gospel through the church in the world.

Living in Europe in the twenty-first century may not feel like God is growing his church very powerfully. But it is still true that he does.

Signs to be hopeful

We live in a unique time. The first half of the twenty-first century in Europe is seeing changes that are unparalleled in history. This affects the church and how we are seeking to see a movement of the gospel in our generation. God is doing something. There are signs and opportunities for it. I believe there are many reasons to be hopeful:

Spiritual Generation

The twentieth century was shaped by the idea of secularisation. Like in many typical science fiction stories, Star Trek is a version of a future world that is totally secular without religions. The idea was that through science humans will say that religion is overcome. That idea itself has passed. Many studies show that today people are interested in spirituality and see it as an important part of their life. This is why our time is called post-secular.

This is a very encouraging reality. In Europe, people are interested in spirituality. We as the church of Jesus have great things to offer. We could be experts for people on a spiritual journey. Our challenge is to engage with them in a fresh way. If we do that well, there are vast opportunities. The harvest is plentiful. May God send workers into our field.

Urban Generation

At the beginning of the twentieth century about 3% of all humans lived in cities. Since 2012 more than 50% live in urban areas. Humanity is moving into the cities. For the first time in world history, the majority is in cities. Predictions show that this will continue.

This development presents a huge opportunity for the church. Our faith is strong in urban places. In the first centuries, the church was mainly a city-movement. Paul went to the urban centres of his time, Ephesus, Korinth, Rome, and others, and it

caused a gospel movement. The gospel includes the hope that one day we will live with God in a great city that will come down from heaven. Augustin explained the church as the city of God being a part of the city of men. Church history proved that the church can do well in cities. I believe that the urban age is not a threat, but a hopeful opportunity for the gospel to be spread and the church to grow. This is a foreshadowing of our eternal super urban future.

Multicultural Generation

Europe has always been a place where different people groups moved around and mixed a lot. Through globalisation and other factors, we see an increase of different cultures living together in many parts of Europe today. The racism and nationalistic ideas of the early 20th century have proved to be wrong. Diversity begins to work. Even though there are serious and alarming streams of anti-multicultural ideologies, the reality in many places in Europe is diverse.

This is a very encouraging factor for a movement of the gospel. Church, from its very beginnings at Pentecost, has been a multicultural crowd. We have a message that unites and is pointing to an eternal future that will be perfectly multicultural. The church can thrive in multicultural settings.

Digital Generation

One of the major changes we are witnessing is digitalization. With significant steps like the Internet, smartphones, and AI the world today is significantly different than two generations ago. It is hard to predict what the world will look like two generations from now. We are still learning what that means and how we can use it well.

Even though there are big challenges and problems to face in the digital world, I believe there are real opportunities for the church. The digital world offers massive chances of communicating the gospel in so many ways. The gospel is a message that has often spread with new developments. When in the fifteenth century book printing was invented (which many refer to as a comparably significant step) it turned out to be a very powerful tool for a movement of gospel - the Reformation. I am optimistic that God will use the opportunities. He will use his church in new ways to reach a digital generation with the good old gospel.

Generation Collaboration

For centuries, the church in Europe was known to be divided. New denominations were started to be different or against the others. Many wars were fought because of this. It caused an enormous amount of pain and gave the church a terrible reputation. Thankfully it seems that this time of conflict and competition is fading. A growing group of church leaders is more open and actively seeking ways to collaborate. The emphasis on the united but diverse Kingdom of God is growing. The task of seeing a movement of the gospel in Europe seems so big that we need to work together and collaborate.

Jesus prayed for his people to be united. He even described unity as a sign of his presence in the world. A church in Europe that is collaborating more and more will be a strong reason to be hopeful that we will see a movement of the gospel.

Living the vision

God gave a vision to the church. His vision. From the beginning, the church was defined and driven by it. This vision is still alive and real. It is still the vision God has, also in Europe. There are signs and areas of opportunity that give much reason for hope.

The vision Jesus gave to his disciples affected them. It made them brave, patient, and God-glorifying.

Brave

After Jesus went to Heaven and the church was born on Pentecost, the followers of Jesus began in a supernaturally brave way to share the gospel. Regardless of hate, misunderstanding, persecution, and death, the church began to act on that vision. It made them brave.

A church in Europe that is driven by this vision will be brave. People will share the gospel not scared of what others will think. People will be very innovative about finding new ways to share the gospel. The church will be outward-focused to be a witness to many. Many new churches will be started and multiplied. The gospel will roll through our countries and cities.

Patient

In the same way, the gospel made people like Paul very relaxed. They had to wait in prison for years. They experienced pushbacks, divisions, challenges, and personal tragedies. For them, it often felt like it was not going so well and not being effective. And that is probably normal in God's Kingdom. But reading the New Testament you never see them in panic. They knew that God was in control, fulfilling his vision.

A church in Europe with God's big vision will be relaxed, patient, and relying on God and his timing. People will share the gospel knowing that it may take a while to bear fruit. Leaders will focus not just on fast results and big numbers, but on a gospel culture.

Churches will get planted, not rushing, but built on long-term health. People will not be crushed when they experience failures.

God-glorifying

In a gospel movement driven by God's vision, you can find people who are brave and relaxed at the same time. They will put all their focus and efforts into seeing this vision realised. But they will leave the timing and results to God.

I am hopeful that we will see a movement of the gospel in Europe. I see the signs. It is already happening. Not always on large scales. Often it feels fragile and imperfect. But that is exactly how God works. And this is how the gospel thrives.

Let us be people and churches with a godly vision for Europe today.

NOTES

Partners

Support us
Give what this is worth to you

This workbook is offered to you for free. We want to continue in this way, and you can support it.

Scan to give

EXURL.EU/GIVE

Printed in Great Britain
by Amazon